For more information about child safety, about abuse and molestation prevention, and about how you can help make children safer and more secure, send a self-addressed, stamped envelope to Children's Institute International, 711 South New Hampshire Avenue, Los Angeles, California 90005.

It Isn't Fair!

A Book About Sibling Rivalry

By Barbara Shook Hazen
Illustrated by Carolyn Bracken

Prepared with the cooperation of Bernice Berk, Ph.D.,
of the Bank Street College of Education

A GOLDEN BOOK · NEW YORK
Western Publishing Company, Inc., Racine, Wisconsin 53404

Note to Parents

A discussion of sibling rivalry (after it has gone over all the fears and anxieties suffered by children who have been presented with a little brother or sister), in the end comes down to a question of love. One of the reasons children are so upset by a new sibling is because they want their parents to love them. They're afraid they might lose that love to someone else. After it becomes clear that the new arrival is here to stay, and as the new sibling grows older, both children become rivals for their parent's undivided love.

Since most parents love their children very much, once this rivalry begins in earnest, they may try to make everyone happy. Sometimes they end up making everyone miserable instead. Parents don't want to make the older child feel displaced, but on the other hand, they don't want the younger child to feel deprived of his or her family rights, either. It may appear on the surface that sibling rivalry is a no-win situation.

But, here again, although fear of loss of love is the cause, love can be the cure. Parents can make it clear to *both* children that the love they feel for their children is something that will never go away. Love isn't like a pie that gets divided up. It is also not diminished by being given freely. Feelings of envy and jealousy during this time are normal, and shouldn't be suppressed artificially.

Children with siblings may want the exclusive love of their parents, but that is something they cannot have. Children have a right to, and usually get, the love of both their parents, and will probably always have that love. But parents must try not to encourage their children's rivalries with each other to be favorite in the family, or to enhance achievement (for example, "Why can't you be like your brother? *He* does his homework!"). In the end, children will only fail to achieve the security of being accepted for themselves. And not only that, there will be a lot of noise and misery on top of it all.

Of course, there will always be some fights and disagreements. But parents should try to avoid putting themselves in judgmental positions that will end up looking like favoritism. That can help keep the situation from escalating. It's often better to make it clear that there is not much to be gained from either parent for the children to be constantly fighting with each other.

—The Editors

A ndy lived in a family where nothing was fair. He had a brother named Scott, who was bigger, which was what *he* wanted to be.

It wasn't fair that Scott got all the grown-up stuff. He even had a brand-new bike.

Andy got baby stuff and had to ride Scott's old bike.

It also wasn't fair that Scott got to stay up late,

and was allowed to cross Main Street by himself, which meant he could go places Andy couldn't.

It wasn't fair that Scott always made up the rules when he and Andy played games.

But when he had a friend over, he put up keep-out signs and wouldn't let Andy play at all.

But what was even more unfair was that his mother and his father both acted like they loved Scott more—or so Andy sometimes felt.

They were always saying how wonderful Scott was,

or making a big deal of going to Scott's Little League games.

Scott also lived in a family where nothing was fair. His little brother, Andy, messed up his stuff. Once, Andy broke the wing of Scott's model airplane and then went off yelling to their mother, "Scott won't share."

That got Scott into trouble, because he was supposed to set a good example.

It wasn't fair that Scott got stuck with all the hard chores around the house.
Andy got the easy stuff.

Sometimes Scott got stuck with Andy, which wasn't fair either.

When Scott and Andy fought, Scott always got blamed because he was bigger and was supposed to know better, which also wasn't fair.

What their mother didn't know was that it was always
Andy who started it, by kicking Scott first or licking the
tops of all the chocolates.

But what was most unfair, or so Scott sometimes thought, was that his mother and father loved Andy more than they loved him.

It seemed like that because his mother picked on him more than she picked on Andy, and because his father still carried Andy on his shoulders at parades. That meant Scott had to walk, which meant he missed some of the good stuff—and his father didn't seem to care about how *he* felt about that.

His mother and father both made a big deal of what a talented artist Andy was, and hung up his dumb pictures all over the place.

Andy and Scott both had a new baby sister, which they
both felt was really unfair.

Because of her, Scott had to share his room with Andy.
Because of her, they both had to be quiet sometimes and
both got blamed when they weren't.

She got more toys than either of them, and couldn't play with any of them.

She got more attention than either of them, and got praised for throwing up.

Times like that, Scott and Andy slam-banged out of house together, and were glad they had each other to do things with and talk about how unfair everything was.

Times like that, they felt like friends, and were glad they were brothers.

There were other times, too.
Andy liked having a big brother who showed him how to do things, like how to hit better,

and who protected him from bullies like Big Bert.

Scott liked having a little brother who looked up to him and wanted to be like him,

and who *was* fun to be with—except when he was a pest.

Way down deep, Andy and Scott loved each other and were glad they were brothers, even when they didn't get along.

They were glad they lived in the same family, and that the baby did too, because once in a while, she was kind of cute.

Way down deep they also knew their parents didn't
love anybody more, but loved each child for his special,
one-of-a-kind self.
Which was good, even if it wasn't always fair.